It is highly doubtful the reigning Spanish kings of the 17th century could have remotely imagined that the extraordinary wealth they were greedily plundering from the inhabitants of the New World for the Spanish Crown was to become the focus of a new nation's struggle for its citizens' rights to private enterprise. Nor could one man, who simply wanted the freedom to go treasure hunting, foresee that he would become the motivation behind a decades-long legal battle that would reaffirm that new nation's fundamental freedoms through the highest court in the land.

THE
ATOCHA
Odyssey

BY PAT CLYNE

A SPECIAL DEDICATION

In loving memory of

Susan Dietrich Clyne

Wife; mother; working professional
Beyond the smoke and rubble—love flourishes
May we never forget 9/11

• • •

Deo Fisher
&
Little Michael Abt

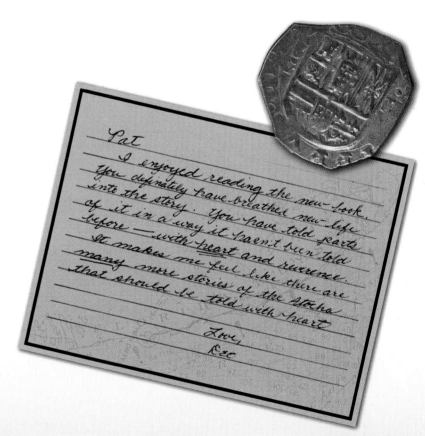

© 2010 Designed in USA by Terrell Creative • Printed in China • 10B0042

ISBN 13: 978-1-56944-406-1

Front and Back Dust Jacket underwater scenic and treasure photos © Pat Clyne and diver with silver bar photo © Don Kincaid; Page 1 artwork, *Francisco Pizarro and his Conquistadors* by Severino Baraldi (b. 1930) Private Collection © Look and Learn/The Bridgeman Art Library, *Golden Doubloon* photo courtesy Fisher Family Collection, Mel Fisher portrait © Mel Fisher's Treasures, Supreme Court photo © Don Kincaid and treasure photos © Pat Clyne; Chapter 1 opener photos courtesy Fisher Family Collection; Chapter 2 opener photos underwater gold bars © Pat Clyne and silver bars in basket photo © Damien Lin; Chapter 3 opener photos © Pat Clyne. Unless otherwise noted, all photos © Pat Clyne.

Text written by Pat Clyne

"Treasure is where you find it!"
cheers,
Pat Clyne

10-23-18
Durod Culpepper
Alabama Crew
1970 - 2001

Table of Contents

Nothing happens unless first a dream.
—CARL SANDBURG

As kids, we found the world a fascinating place to explore. Intricacies of the planet were best left for the "grown-ups." Things were either good or bad; school was tolerated; Cap'n Crunch, ice cream and candy were the basic food groups; and searching for lost treasure—well, that's just what we wanted to do for the rest of our lives.

Then we grew up; discovered gray areas; found that education was important; eating "green" things was healthy; and lost treasure—well, that was just a fantasy that was best left for kids to dream about. We all know "grown-ups" wouldn't dream of that ... would they?

The
Formative
Years

ot even a child would think it's a good idea to put a bucket over their head, weight themselves down, then walk into a lake while having a friend force air down to them through a bicycle pump. The exception to that seemingly reasonable logic was in the mind of a young Mel Fisher. He thought it out, and logically to him, it would work. Still, most people, young or old, would wonder why anyone would even want to take that chance. Like the first person to ever try eating an oyster or climb into a space capsule, those puzzling uncertainties can only have been answered by those who take the first plunge—that giant leap into the mysterious unknown. The results of such endeavors could lead to tremendous disaster or great success. Of course, we would never know if we let that chance—or is it opportunity?—pass us by. Sometimes it takes a special individual to make that first move. This is the story about such a man and his family who believed that he and others in this country had the right to take those chances and turn them into opportunities.

Even as a child, Mel had the knack of persuading people to take chances. Not only would it be okay, but in the end they would feel better about themselves for just trying. Mel Fisher's gift was that not only would he be the first to attempt new ventures but that he could foster that belief in others. This was a talent that would play a huge role in Mel Fisher's success as a leader of men in the quest for adventure, exploration and discovery.

Mel Fisher was born on August 21st, 1922 in Hobart, Indiana to Earl Fisher, a hard-working carpenter and his mother Grace

Photo courtesy Fisher Family Collection

Photo courtesy Fisher Family Collection

Photo courtesy Fisher Family Collection

Spencel, who along with her sisters, came from a talented musical family. This melodical flair was not to be lost on young Melvin. His childhood seemed to follow the normal boyhood expectations of cuts and scrapes, playing hooky and getting into the usual "boy" trouble. Although he was an above-average student, many of his unconventional childhood exploits led some to think that young Melvin Fisher was not entirely dealing in reality. They would mistake his intense curiosity about how things could be done differently as stubborn adolescence.

As a child, Mel could create and play out in his mind an assortment of simple and complex fantasies, all of which might have very well concluded in "happy endings." Maybe it was because he dealt with those obstacles and overcame them in childhood that success to him in later years was already a foregone conclusion. This is perhaps oversimplifying Mel Fisher's astounding optimism, but it just might also explain some of his more visionary exploits in the years to come.

An avid reader of adventure novels, young Mel soon became intrigued with the works of Robert Louis Stevenson and his portrayal of the Spanish Main, hidden treasure and pirates. His

Shortstop Mel Fisher, age 4 **(above)**

Cowpoke Mel Fisher, age 6 **(left)**

Mel Fisher, age 8 months; Bear, expired **(opposite page)**

PHONE 4726

MUSIC FOR ALL OCCASIONS

MEL FISHER
A. F. OF M. BOOKING AGENT

DELTA CHI FRATERNIT
351 NORTHWESTERN

PHONE 4-4195

MELODY MASTERS
DANCE ORCHESTRA
LARGE OR SMALL ORCHESTRA
REASONABLE RATES

GARY, INDIANA

4091 FILLMORE ST.

Mel Fisher's two bands—The Melody
Masters & The Mel Fisher Orchestra
(above left and right)

favorite would be *Treasure Island*, and he would spend hours reading and rereading passages that seemed to whisk him away into the mind of young Jim Hawkins, through which Mel viewed this new fantasy, replete with adventure, danger, greed and riches. Mel's fervent imagination made *Treasure Island* a whimsical playground. It was also an adolescent's introduction to the age-old conflict of good versus evil. How would he, the young Mel Fisher, have handled Long John Silver?

While attending Lew Wallace High School in Glen Park Indiana, Mel developed his talent as a musician and formed his first band. By the time he went off to study engineering in college at Purdue University, his musical skills earned him his own dance band appropriately named The Mel Fisher's Melody Masters. His band became a successful and very popular replication of the big swing bands of that era. In his Delta Chi Fraternity and around Gary, Indiana his Melody Masters became a household name.

His love for the saxophone would follow him throughout his life; it wasn't uncommon to see Mel Fisher up on stage in a nightclub playing a lilting rendition of "Sentimental Journey," a classic instrumental that would become his and his wife's favorite song.

Because of his engineering background, Mel was recruited into the Army Corps of Engineers during World War II. After a stint in Europe in the military, Mel returned to the U.S. to help move his family to Torrance, California to begin life as a chicken farmer. Although he studied animal husbandry at El Camino College, it's not certain that Mel Fisher actually had his heart set on making this his career. When asked about his former occupation, he would exclaim, "Besides cleaning out the pens and keepin' 'em fed, there wasn't much else to do; the chickens did most of the work; they just kept right on poopin'

out those eggs." It appeared that Mel was just not convinced that sitting around waiting for chickens to "poop eggs" was what he wanted to do for the rest of his life.

However, fate was now to play an important role in his life when the family chicken farm was sold to a Montana family. It was then that Mel met and fell head-over-heels in love with a beautiful young redhead named Dolores Horton, the daughter of one of the new chicken ranch owners. Dolores would soon discover that Mel Fisher was not just your average egg-collecting, straw-chewing, pooper-scooping chicken farmer.

The two hit it off immediately and soon became inseparable. It wasn't long after, that Mel and "Deo," (as she was affectionately known), discovered they were soul mates. So they took the plunge (pun intended), and were married in California in 1953. They were now about to embark on a journey that Mel promised her would be a lifetime of "Fun, Romance and Adventure." Around that same time, Jacques Cousteau's new underwater device called the Aqua-Lung was becoming very popular among the more adventurous types. This steel cylinder was carried on a diver's back supplying him air through a

Mel serving in the U.S. Army Corps of Engineers **(above)**

Knotty Pine Chicken Ranch— Judith, Evalyn and Deo Horton pictured from left to right **(left)**

Photo courtesy Fisher Family Collection

Mel Fisher with lobster **(above)**

Mel with his newly invented underwater camera case **(right)**

mouthpiece attached to a hose from the cylinder. This new invention was called SCUBA, an acronym for Self Contained Underwater Breathing Apparatus, and it was starting to become very popular as a sport in Europe. Mel, who was already an avid skin diver, thought this 'SCUBA' fad might catch on in California also, so he bought an air compressor, filled scuba tanks and created homemade dive gear working out of one of his feed sheds on the ranch.

OUT OF THE HENHOUSE AND INTO THE DEEP

Mel introduced his formerly landlocked Montana bride to the wonders and beauty of the sea, both above and under it. Deo took to her new world as any newborn mermaid would ... she was a natural. On their honeymoon they went shipwreck diving in the Florida Keys, a place they loved at first sight but never dreamed at the time would eventually play such a pivotal role in shaping their future.

When they returned to California they decided to build a dive shop. It would be the first of its kind anywhere and Mel and Deo would pioneer it. But, finances being scarce, in order to raise

Photo courtesy Fisher Family Collection

Phone FRontier 5-6714

Movies Underwater

MEL FISHER   1911 SO. CATALINA AVE.
REDONDO BEACH, CALIFORNIA

money to build the shop, they would dive for lobsters and sell them off one by one. Mel would say, "Every lobster we caught bought us another brick for the store." He would joke that it was "the only building in the world ever built completely from lobster tails."

Mel's Aqua Shop in Redondo Beach, California was finally opened, and he and Deo began teaching scuba lessons, taking divers on shipwreck dives and undersea excursions. They also led weekend fortune hunters into the rivers of California panning for gold. Mel soon became an expert in spearfishing and hauled to the surface many fish bigger than he was. Ever the entrepreneur, Mel devised an underwater housing for his

16mm Bell & Howell movie camera that he took with him on his dive exploits. He would edit and narrate the film that he produced as a series of adventure stories featured on his own local television channel, and eventually, even in Hollywood. This spawned more interest in the sport and a new generation of wanna-be divers would flock to Mel's Aqua Shop to learn to become certified "frogmen."

Deo, too, not only participated in all of these activities, but in 1959 took this new diving "fad" a step further. Fifty-five hours, 37 minutes and 9.6 seconds after she submerged in a pool with scuba gear, Deo Fisher surfaced with a new underwater endurance world record. It might have been one small dip for a lady, but it certainly proved to be one giant plunge for womankind. For that and many other groundbreaking achievements, Deo became one of the first honorees to be inducted into the coveted Women's Diving Hall of Fame, a prestigious organization that recognizes the lifetime achievements of its nominees. She is also featured, along with her husband, in the *Who's Who Of Diving* as well as a host of other prominent tributes befitting her celebrated career.

Deo Fisher resting while setting the underwater scuba endurance record **(above)**

Deo Fisher advertises her upcoming record dive attempt. **(above top)**

Deo Horton Fisher **(left)**

Photo courtesy Fisher Family Collection

The Fisher Family: Mel, Kane,
Dirk, Deo and Kim **(above)**

Dirk, Kane and Kim Fisher **(above right)**

Mel's Aqua Shop Ad **(right)**

Photo by Chuck Peterson courtesy Fisher Family Collection

Mel and Deo began filming commercials for a leading bathing suit company whose success today continues as a result of Deo Fisher's early modeling career, which prompted thousands of women to get "the look" to impress their men while sunbathing at the beach. Besides filming his own movies and producing a popular weekly television show, Mel was asked to perform in front of the camera as well. Shows like *High Road To Danger* and various other thrill-seeking adventure forums would request the Fishers to film and serialize their lifestyle.

Contrary to popular belief, Mel and Deo did not spend *all* of their time underwater. By 1954, the pitter-patter of little web feet could be heard around the pool. The Fishers had eventually expanded their family to include four more future aquanauts. Three sons, Dirk, Kim and Kane were born and lastly, making her debut, was daughter Taffi, who perfectly balanced out the clan. All of them learned to swim and dive as quickly as most kids learn to walk. The Fisher offspring were to play prominent roles in their parents' quest; they were all to become an integral part of the Mel Fisher saga and make possible his passage into history.

THE SEARCH FOR SUNKEN TREASURE

While Mel and Deo were busy building a dive business and a family in California, another pioneer, Kip Wagner was discovering the remains of some Spanish galleons on Florida's east coast. A fleet of treasure ships heading back to Spain loaded with New World riches were caught in a ferocious hurricane in 1715. Twelve ships, with their precious cargoes of gold, silver and jewelry, and hundreds of lives were all lost on Florida's eastern shores.

Kip organized a group of divers to begin diving on these wrecks. Since all of the men had other full-time jobs, it was more of a weekend diving stint. However, as Kip and the others began finding more treasure, their passion and incentive grew so much that they formed a treasure hunting business called the "Real Eight Company." The genie of entrepreneurship for historical marine salvage was out of the bottle. Now with the advent of scuba, the wonders beneath the ocean's surface were accessible to anyone who had the desire to explore it.

Hundreds of years of our history and culture were lying unseen and slowly deteriorating just a few hundred yards off the beach. And now, American ingenuity and a few 20th-century explorers were about to change that.

The notion that there were valuable shipwrecks lying undiscovered on the ocean's bottom was not one that escaped Mel

Bernard Romans' Map of 1775. This is one of the earliest references indicating the names and location of each wreck site. **(above)**

ed to pursue a dream. So when Kip invited Mel to move to Florida and join him in the hunt, Mel didn't have to be asked twice. However, there was just one small thing he needed to do first, and that was to convince Deo they should sell everything and move the whole family across the country to go treasure hunting. Well, why not? It made perfect sense to Mel Fisher. Mel, who as a child convinced his best friend that he wouldn't drown walking into a lake with a bucket on his head, now had to utilize all of his persuasive skills for the biggest sell of his life. But Mel, as always, had a plan. When he got back to California, he collected up all of the household bills—mortgage, utility, car bills, etc.—along with boat costs, dive store inventory and every other debit receipt he could get his hands on. He piled them all up on the kitchen table and invited Deo to join him in trying to figure out how they were going to handle all of these expenses. Admittedly, the mountain of bills looked overwhelming and the task extremely depressing. So Mel said to her, "Honey, wouldn't you rather go treasure hunting than to have to deal with all of that?" Mel, of course, already knew there could only be one answer to that type of logic. How

Fisher either. He had already purchased a dive boat that he named *Golden Doubloon* and began searching the California coast, Panama and Silver Shoals for shipwrecks. So, when Mel heard of this other like-minded explorer who was finding treasures from Spanish wrecks on the east coast, he made a special trip to Florida to meet with him.

Kip Wagner and Mel Fisher hit it off right away, both entertaining each other with tales of their underwater exploits. It was obvious to Mel that Kip was on to something big; it was obvious to Kip that Mel had the optimism and spirit that was need-

Golden Doubloon **(above)**

could Deo refuse? Well, she didn't. The strategy worked perfectly, and they started making plans right away.

Mel also wanted to convince a few of his dive buddies to join him on his venture. However, he didn't have any money to pay them. So, he made a deal with them. If within one year of starting their expedition they didn't hit it big, they would return home. Mel's team also bought into his logic and signed onto the quest. They formed a company called Cobb Coin Co. and packed for the journey. After selling their home, their boat and their dive shop business, the Fisher family expedition loaded up all their worldly possessions, piled the kids into their old station wagon and headed across the country to follow their dream.

"ARE WE THERE YET?"

Anyone who has had the "pleasure" of going on an all-day field trip with a car full of kids would appreciate Mel and Deo's cross-country drive. If this was a test of their patience for things to come, then they had passed it masterfully; not one drop of blood was shed, and they all arrived safely at their destination in Sebastian, Florida eager to begin the search. It was

1963 and a new chapter in Florida's colorful history was about to be written.

Like most projects, this one had its unforeseen problems. Since many of the ships in the 1715 fleet grounded and broke up close to shore, the wave action and tidal currents in the relatively shallow waters were factors to which the divers were not accustomed. Also, the turbulence caused the bottom sediment to be churned up creating limited visibility. How were the divers supposed to find treasure when they couldn't even see each other? Mel reasoned that if the top layer of clear water could

Mel and Deo on the newly completed *Golden Doubloon*, a Spanish galleon replica. **(above)**

Diagram of Mel's mailboxes **(above)**

somehow be propelled to the bottom, then the divers would be able to see what they were doing. The theory made sense, but just how does one go about transporting thousands of gallons of clear water to the bottom of the ocean? Mel's years of engineering experience were now about to be put to the test.

Many times throughout his career when the going got really tough, he would be asked why he continued to keep taking on these seemingly impossible tasks. He would often just smile and say, "If it were easy, everyone would be doing it." Mel believed in himself and that self-assurance was apparent, so much so, that most people who have ever worked with him would tell you that if it weren't for Mel's continued cheerful optimism and good spirits, they would have quit long ago. After all, it did seem to them that anyone who was that positive had to know something they didn't—right?

The year was almost up, and Mel's team had not yet hit it "big." They had all but exhausted their finances and needed to get back to their real jobs. It looked to many of them as though it would soon be over—but hey!—they didn't regret it. They did what many people only dream they could do. At least now they would have glorious tales to tell their kids and grandkids. For most of them, the adventure itself was worth it. Mel was entertaining ideas also, but quitting wasn't one of them. He and one of his scientist-turned-diver friends, Fay Field, had just developed a concept on how to solve the visibility problem. They devised an aluminum-shaped tube with a 90-degree elbow that when lowered over a propeller could deflect the propwash downward to the bottom. They designed and made a prototype to try on one of their vessels. Someone mentioned that the configuration resembled a large mailbox; the name somehow stuck and is still used today to describe Mel's invention. Mel and his crew went out to test his new "mailbox" device. The divers anchored their salvage boat just a short distance from shore and placed the "mailbox" behind the boat's propeller. A diver got in the water and swam to the bottom

while another throttled the engine to increase the prop's rpm. Mel's simple but ingenious plan worked. The clear water from the surface was pushed to the bottom and visibility increased dramatically. The divers were elated, but not just about the clear water on the bottom. They also discovered that the deflected propwash had another astounding effect. It was moving large portions of sand away. The task of hand fanning the sand for hours at a time to locate artifacts could now be done in a fraction of the time. The search for buried treasure now took on a new and exciting perspective.

Time, however, was still running out. After a hard day of diving, the salvors would put in extra hours in the evening at the machine shop building a bigger mailbox for deeper water. They were convinced that Mel's invention would uncover what they set out to find almost a year earlier. With just days left to their working agreement, they sailed to an area where they had found some traces of wreckage but were unable to dig any further through the deep sand. They lowered the large mailbox over the prop of their salvage vessel while divers hovered beneath it. The engine was turned on and a surge of water pushed the divers

Deo displays an encrusted silver plate. **(above)**

Deo and Dirk working the 1715 fleet. **(left)**

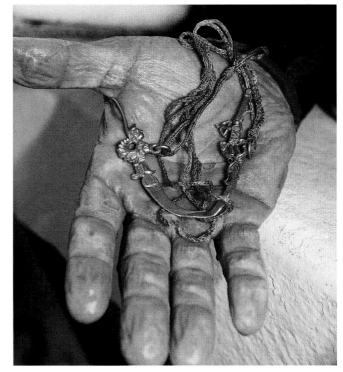

straight to the bottom, but unlike previous dives, they could now see what was happening around them, and what was happening was a sight that few people could ever imagine, let alone experience.

The water pressure from the propeller's downward thrust was removing the sand right under their noses. As the sand dispersed on all sides of them, they found themselves in the center of an aquatic vortex of swirling water and surreal images. Their eyes were affixed to the ever-widening hole as round shiny objects began to appear from all sides of the deepening cavity. Suddenly, the divers completely forgot that they were riding an underwater rollercoaster and instead focused on the new reality of being completely surrounded by hundreds of gold coins. They had just astonishingly met their deadline!

Mel Fisher's Cobb Coin Company and Kip Wagner's Real Eight Company made headlines around the world. When asked what it was like to find sunken treasure, Mel would reflect on that one historic dig that produced over a thousand gold doubloons and say, "Once you've seen the ocean bottom paved with gold, you'll never forget it." So it was, with the advent of Mel's new "mailboxes" that the salvors went on to retrieve, from deep in the submerged sands of Florida's rich coastline, the hidden cargoes of those lost galleons, and to preserve for us that rich history from which the secrets of our past can finally be revealed.

For some people, success like that might make one consider an early retirement. But for Mel and his family, the satisfaction of sticking with something they believed in, as well as the challenges they met, made the journey worthwhile. As far as accomplishing this masterful feat, for Mel Fisher and his family, it just meant they could do it again.

Gold filigree locket **(above)**
Gold scimitar toothpicks **(above right)**

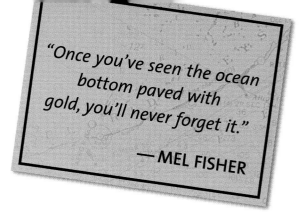

"Once you've seen the ocean bottom paved with gold, you'll never forget it."

—MEL FISHER

Photo courtesy Fisher Family Collection

Photo © Pat Clyne

Diver deposits handful of gold coins on boat before returning for more. **(above)**

Gold coins from the 1715 fleet **(left)**

The Atocha and the Florida Keys

One shipwreck in particular caught the eye of many fortune seekers —The *Nuestra Señora de Atocha*. Its cargo of riches from the New World exceeded any other in Potter's book and its location seemed within reach. Potter indicated that the *Atocha* and her sister ship, *Santa Margarita*, could be found off the lower Matecumbe Keys, a group of islands easily accessible along U.S. 1, also called The Overseas Highway. Given Mel's success on the 1715 fleet, it was only a matter of time before he would undertake what could arguably be the most ambitious expedition of the 20th century—the one that would confirm, for all time, Mel Fisher's title of —*"The World's Greatest Treasure Hunter."*

THE TREASURE DIVER'S GUIDE

INCLUDING LOCATIONS OF SUNKEN TREASURES; TECHNIQUES OF RESEARCH, SEARCH, AND SALVAGE; WRECK IDENTIFICATION; AND SUBMARINE ARCHAEOLOGY

Published in 1972, Doubleday (Garden City, N.Y.)

Mel and Dr. Eugene Lyon studying research materials **(above)**

The Treasure Diver's Guide by John Potter **(above middle)**

Mel Fisher points to spot on *Atocha* site. **(above right)**

*M*el Fisher's success in locating and recovering a significant portion of the 1715 Spanish fleet brought him worldwide recognition along with the celebrated title of "The World's Greatest Treasure Hunter." This label, Mel Fisher soon learned, required constant maintenance.

Author and researcher John Potter published a book in the early 1960s cataloguing historic shipwrecks. Many treasure hunters considered *The Treasure Diver's Guide* as the bible of treasure wrecks and where they might be found. But Potter's locations of many of these ships were approximate at best.

The year was 1968, and Mel was now convinced he was going to be the one to locate the *Atocha*—and he would do it in six months. Well, at least he was half right. Mel would readily admit that one of the secrets of his success was to surround himself with "good" people. Mostly, these were people who had like interests, although he sometimes found people (or they found him) with interests outside of treasure hunting whose skills he felt could adapt to the search. One such person was

Gene Lyon, a scholar of Spanish history who was also a member of Mel and Deo's church in Vero Beach. Mel knew that Gene, a PhD candidate, was conducting research in the archives of Seville, Spain which is a repository of original ancient documents. Mel also knew many of these were accounts of lost Spanish vessels, their cargoes and the attempt by Spain to salvage them. Mel realized early on that Gene could be the one person on his team who could actually define a more precise location for the *Atocha*.

Gene Lyon was now to become Mel's eyes and ears into the past. With Gene's research, Mel now had a lead over the other treasure hunters searching for the *Atocha* in the lower Matecumbes. Gene had translated documents confirming that the Spaniards at that time had considered *all* of the Florida Keys as "Matecumbe." That new information led to a startling revelation. Potter's guide, although grammatically correct in its translation, did not take into account the Spanish names for their actual geographic locations. Gene had discovered the one

important clue that none of the other treasure hunters had, and that clue told Mel Fisher that his competitors were all searching over a hundred miles away in the wrong place.

Mel's confidence in Gene Lyon's research was apparent as he packed up his family and his new company, Treasure Salvors, Inc. and moved them all to Key West to continue their search. It was now 1970, and with this new research, Mel was confident that he would locate the *Atocha* any day now. His optimism was becoming contagious.

Another member of Mel's team was scientist Fay Field who developed an underwater metal detector called a proton magnetometer. The "mag," as it was called, could be towed by a boat to locate metal and iron objects on the ocean floor. This was an excellent tool to locate cannons, anchors and assorted ferrous objects strewn about the seabed. However, it was also an excellent tool to locate hundreds of years of metal junk also lying on the bottom. But that little fact never deterred Mel. As he told his divers many times after making hundreds of dives on countless pieces of metal debris, "Hey, look at it this way, ya only gotta be right once."

While the "mag" was being towed behind their search vessel, one of Mel's divers could be seen standing on an improvised tower that was strategically placed at sea. The "fryboy," as he was called, would watch the "mag" boat through a telescope, which had a built-in compass. This was known as a theodolite, and it tracked the boat's vertical position from the tower. The idea was for the fryboy to keep the search boat on course by radio communication before the sun could propel him into various stages of hallucination. It was a delicate balancing act and a credit to his endurance that would not go unrewarded. He returned back to Key West with a much improved suntan, compliments of his on-the-job-training.

Photo © Pat Clyne

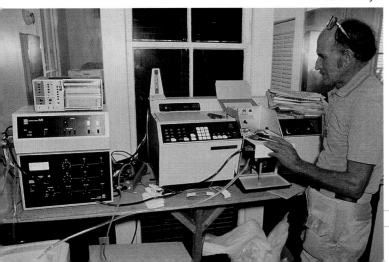

Photo © Pat Clyne

Theodolite operator, Charlie Clyne, tracks a search vessel and corrects its course by radio from this tower. **(above)**

Fay Field, electronics expert and developer of the seagoing Proton Magnetometer, operates atomic absorption photo spectrometer. **(left)**

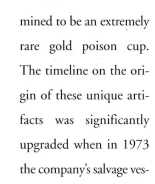

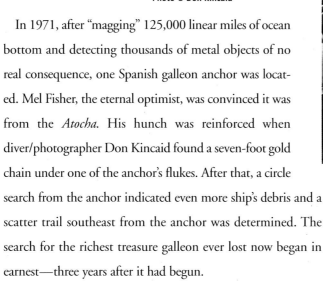

The first anchor, found in 1972, turned out to be from the *Atocha*. **(above)**

Don Kincaid holds the gold chain found under the *Atocha* anchor. **(above left)**

Dirk with astrolabe **(above middle)**

Gold poison cup found by Kim Fisher **(above right)**

THE FIRST CLUES

In 1971, after "magging" 125,000 linear miles of ocean bottom and detecting thousands of metal objects of no real consequence, one Spanish galleon anchor was located. Mel Fisher, the eternal optimist, was convinced it was from the *Atocha*. His hunch was reinforced when diver/photographer Don Kincaid found a seven-foot gold chain under one of the anchor's flukes. After that, a circle search from the anchor indicated even more ship's debris and a scatter trail southeast from the anchor was determined. The search for the richest treasure galleon ever lost now began in earnest—three years after it had begun.

Shortly after the recovery of the anchor, Mel's oldest son Dirk, captain of one of the company's two yellow tugboats, *Northwind*, recovered a bronze astrolabe from the site. This was a navigational device used by the Spaniards to determine their location at sea and a forerunner of the more modern sextant. The astrolabe was in remarkably good condition and was a major discovery.

Not to be outdone, Mel's younger son Kim, captain of the company's sister ship *Southwind*, located what was later deter-

mined to be an extremely rare gold poison cup. The timeline on the origin of these unique artifacts was significantly upgraded when in 1973 the company's salvage vessel, *Virgalona*, captained by Mel's loyal Panamanian friend, Mo (Demontenes Molinar), uncovered over a thousand silver "pieces of eight." So many coins were found that we nicknamed the area "The Bank of Spain."

These Spanish coins, or reales, were in such good condition that after the black sulfide concretion was removed, the Hapsburg Shield of Spain could be seen on one side and the Crusader's, or Jerusalem, cross on the other. What was most noteworthy was that the dates on these coins did not exceed 1622—an important indication that the wreck they were on was indeed part of *Atocha*'s Tierra Firma Fleet of 1622. But with eight ships sunk of the 28 which sailed in the fleet, the question now was: Which ship was it?

THE ATOCHA SILVER BARS

That same year, another important recovery was made by Mel's youngest son Kane, who was only 13 at the time, diving with his buddy, Mike Schnaedelbach. Three large silver bars bearing the King's tax stamps and owner's registry numbers were brought up from an area known on the local nautical charts as the "Quicksands." Now, if Gene Lyon could match the registry numbers with those on the Atocha manifest, Mel would finally have conclusive proof that the shipwreck trail we had been following was indeed that of the *Atocha*.

Mel arranged for a large butcher's scale to be placed on the deck of the company's replica Spanish galleon. As *National Geographic* cameras rolled and the press snapped their pictures, one of the bars, whose registry number matched the manifest, was placed on the scale. If the bar weighed

83 pounds, it would also match the listed manifest weight of that bar … double proof! Everyone held their breath as the needle of the scale bounced back and forth before coming to a stop on that magical number—83! Loud applause and cheers broke the deafening silence while Mel and Deo's smiles spoke volumes. It seemed that Mel had finally been vindicated. Now all his detractors would believe that he had what he set out to find almost four years earlier. Or at least, that's what we all thought.

Some of those detractors however, turned out to be relentless in their denial of Mel's new entitlement. Some insisted that Mel had an entirely different shipwreck and the *Atocha* would still eventually be found in the Matecumbe Keys. Others, through bitterness or jealousy, spread rumors that Mel actually planted the silver bars just to get more investors. When the mainstream press printed nasty articles attributed to Mel's critics, one local journalist, Wendy Tucker, from our hometown newspaper, *The Key West Citizen*, would counter just as hard with rebuttals, along with more positive news on Mel's latest recoveries. Mel could always rely

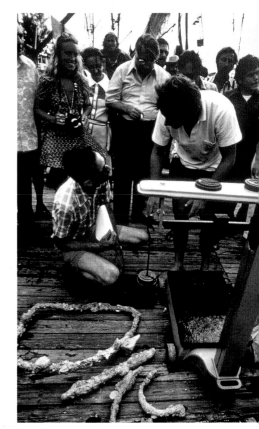

Photo by Don Kincaid

Dr. Eugene Lyon had prepared a scale on the deck of the replica Spanish galleon to weigh what became known as "The Definitive Silver Bar." **(above)**

Markings on the silver bars that matched those on the *Atocha*'s manifest convinced most people that the *Atocha* had been found. **(left)**

on Wendy's counterpoints when confronted with investors who might have read the "wrong" newspaper that day. Throughout it all, Mel's trademark optimism remained unshakable, and he forged ahead. The search continued along that trail with the company's tugboats for three more years.

THE SOUTHWIND

At sixteen, most teenage boys are out cruising in their parent's car scouting for 16-year-old girls—not so for Kim Fisher. Mel and Deo's second son was the captain of one of the company's large yellow tugboats and was cruising the Florida Straits looking for Spanish galleons. Kim stood 6'3" and had long yellow hair that hung to his mid-back. Most of us on the *Southwind* were in our twenties and by the standards of the day, we might have been called "hippies." Most of this would be attributed to our non-conformist attire of sandals, cutoff jeans and stylishly torn t-shirts. But even our rag-tag appearance became part of the Fisher mystique.

Just about everything we did was different from conventional procedure. The impossible, our critics would learn, took

Mel's team a little longer, but eventually our "motley crew of misfits," as we had been labeled, would somehow pull it off. This left a lot of government bureaucrats scratching their heads wondering just how far this Fisher guy, his family and crew could go before finally succumbing to government pressure.

Kim and his crew blazed the trail from the galleon anchor through the Quicksands finding some of the *Atocha's* most valuable items between 1972 and 1975. Kim, who was honed on the sea by his parents, was already an experienced seaman and natural leader. His 20th-century exploits along with his crew on the high seas in those formative years would soon rival any swashbuckling folklore of the past. There were many har-

rowing tales of barely escaping danger or even worse. Both *Northwind* and *Southwind* crews had formed a camaraderie that was usually reserved for soldiers on the battlefield. We were confident of our skills, and in emergencies we instinctively knew that our dive buddy "had our back." Our youthful and impetuous slogan upon reaching port after a two-week expedition at sea would be, *"We've cheated death again!"* This slogan would sadly, soon run its course.

THE BRONZE CANNONS

Even though we were finding fascinating and valuable bits and pieces of the *Atocha* cargo, the "Motherlode" of the *Atocha*–47 tons of silver and gold—was still evading us. Mel's chief archaeologist, Duncan Mathewson, had a theory that the *Atocha*'s main cultural deposit, as he liked to call it, might be found further down the trail in deeper water. Dirk Fisher thought this would be an idea worth trying. So he took his vessel *Northwind* and sailed out to test Duncan's deep-water theory.

As Mel and Deo's oldest son, Dirk, more than the rest of his siblings, had watched his mom and dad struggle through their seemingly endless battles with rivals, creditors, boat repairs, weather and of course, government roadblocks. He, like his father, was very strong willed; some would even say stubborn. When Dirk got an idea into his head, he would play it out until he was satisfied with the results. Not many people could talk him out of an idea once he decided to act upon it, not even Mel. So when his father voiced some concern over Duncan's deep-water theory, Dirk's mind was already made up. His father's recollections of the hazards of deep-water diving and the loss of some of his friends on previous expeditions didn't deter Dirk. If there was a chance that the *Atocha* was in deeper water, then that's where Dirk wanted to go.

One morning on the site in July of 1975, Dirk woke early and left the stateroom that he shared with Angel, his attractive blond bride of six months. He climbed topside and looked at the ocean around him. Something didn't seem to be right. The styrofoam buoys they had set the night before to mark their position had moved—or had they? Thinking the *Northwind* had dragged her anchor during the night, Dirk donned a mask and a pair of fins, jumped into the water and

Photo © Pat Clyne

Diver swims by one of nine Bronze cannons. **(above)**

Bronze cannon coming out of water
(above)

Atocha Cannons Site Map **(above top)**

headed for the bottom, 37 feet below. If the anchor had dragged, then there would be no sign of the previous day's work on the seabed. What he saw instead caused him to loose his breath—he began to claw his way to the surface as quick as his fins could propel him.

The *Atocha* was the most prestigious galleon in the entire fleet. It was designated as "Almirante" or guard galleon and took up a position in the rear. The *Atocha* was one of the few galleons of its time to carry large bronze cannons, and Dirk Fisher had always told his crew that if they ever found a bronze cannon it would lead them to the *Atocha*'s resting place. So when Dirk spotted five of these big guns lying on the bottom, piled on top of each other, it literally took his breath away. When he broke the surface, he started yelling at the top of his lungs— "Cannons...we've got bronze cannons!"

The *Northwind* crew, most of whom were just getting out of their bunks, heard Dirk's shouts but couldn't understand what he was yelling. In his jubilance, Dirk was wildly thrashing about in the water and some of the divers began to think he was being attacked by sharks. But that couldn't be the case, they thought.

Nobody who was being attacked by sharks could have that big of a smile on their face. It was beginning to look as though Duncan's theory might be right after all.

Word was radioed back to headquarters in Key West, and a boat was immediately dispatched to the site with Duncan, a Miami film crew and other divers onboard. A photo-grid was placed over the cannons, and archaeological pictures were taken as Duncan documented their location underwater while the rest of us celebrated topside. Could it get any better than this we wondered? Well, yes it could—and it did ... almost twice as good.

The next day, Dirk moved the *Northwind* about thirty feet from the five bronze cannons and began to dust the sand from the bottom using the ship's mailboxes. After a ten-minute blow, he sent divers Jim Solanick and I down to check the area. After the sediment began to settle, the barrels of two more bronze cannons began to stare back at me—a sight I refused to believe until I wrapped my legs around one of them, only wishing I could ride it to the surface. Instead, I swam up and repeated the euphoric scene from the day before as I began yelling, "Two more cannons down there." A few moments later, diver Jim Solanick

Photo © Pat Clyne

surfaced and shouted that he had also found two more cannons. Another four of the big guns had been uncovered. The *Northwind* crew had now located a total of nine bronze cannons.

Mel, Deo and all the rest of us felt that the *Atocha* had finally given up her hiding place, and it would only be a matter of days before the Motherlode, or the "Big Pile" as Mel called it, would be uncovered. The clear markings on the cannons finally proved, even to Mel's most hardened skeptics, that this was, without a doubt, the *Atocha*. It looked as though the Fishers were, after almost seven years of searching, about to reap their big reward. Unfortunately, fate doesn't always follow logic. The whole Fisher team was about to suffer the most incomprehensible tragedy imaginable, and the cannon discovery would ulti-

mately become a footnote to this story instead of one of its most defining moments.

THE TRAGEDY

On the following trip to the wrecksite, the *Northwind* anchored for the night west of the Marquesas Islands. Mel and Deo's youngest son, Kane, was now 16 and joined his older brother, Dirk, whom he idolized. Kane was still in high school, but when he could he would be out on the site with his brothers and diving with the rest of the crew. It was summer vacation and Kane could usually be found somewhere on one of the boats pulling his weight in the family business. On this particular evening after dinner, Dirk hosted a small party for his wife Angel; it was her 28th birthday. The entire crew toasted both of them on a long and prosperous life together, especially now when they all believed that in just a matter of hours they may discover the richest shipwreck in history. However, this celebration didn't last into the night as they sometimes do. Everyone turned in early that night, as they all agreed that the next day was going to be the big one, one that they were sure

Dirk and Angel Fisher a few weeks before their drowning **(above)**

Archaeologist Duncan Mathewson taking transit measurements **(left)**

Virgalona **(above)**

The *Northwind* in dry dock just
before her fatal sinking **(right)**

they would remember for the rest of their lives. How unfortunate that truth was to be.

In the very early hours of the morning, while everyone slept, the *Northwind* began taking on water. When the big yellow tugboat reached the critical stage of list, it abruptly capsized, throwing crew members who were comfortably sleeping on deck one second into a dark wet void the next, while trapping those asleep below in their bunkrooms. Survivors scrambled in the water to reach and cling to the overturned barnacle-encrusted hull of their ship. Some thought they were experiencing a horrible nightmare and prayed to wake up. Others sought out their comrades in the surreal murky chaos. But as the *Northwind's* hull now began to sink below them, they realized that their captain Dirk Fisher, his wife Angel and fellow diver Rick Gage would not be joining them. And so they floated in total darkness—chilled, shivering and bleeding from barnacle cuts—while drifting aimlessly in a sea of oil, diesel fuel and sharks.

Several hours after daybreak, Mo, the captain of the *Virgalona*, headed out to the *Atocha* site from his own anchorage at the Marquesas. He soon spotted an oil slick, debris and what appeared to him as heads bobbing in the water. It was the remainder of the *Northwind* crew. The injured and trembling divers were quickly plucked from the sea, and although traumatized, they began to reveal to a stunned *Virgalona* crew the details of their night of horror.

Mo traced the oil slick back to the *Northwind's* anchor buoy that marked the resting place of the ill-fated vessel. His divers quickly geared up—there was still some hope among the crew that their missing comrades might still be alive and trapped in an air pocket within the ship. Young Kane Fisher sat shivering on the *Virgalona* deck, his mind racing through the night's

Photo © Pat Clyne

frightful events. He was now left with the unimaginable prospect that his oldest brother and mentor might be gone. When the divers reached the hull and penetrated the interior, the scene that greeted them painfully dashed all their hopes. Our comrades; dive buddies; friends; would not be coming home alive this trip.

The bodies of Dirk, Angel and Rick were very carefully recovered by their comrades and in grave sorrow, transported back to Key West where they and the *Virgalona* crew were met at the pier by a grief-stricken Mel and Deo who tearfully hugged each survivor as they disembarked onto the dock. As Kane Fisher embraced his parents, there were no words to say, no comfort to be found—only heartache to be shared as a teenager, who in one night of terror, suffered the worst "rites of passage" a child would have to endure. From that day on, July 20th, 1975, Kane was imbued with inexplicable determination to carry on and fulfill his deceased brother's quest—at all costs.

This was the one and only time in his life that Mel ever had doubts about what to do next. We all became withdrawn as well. The "Fun, Romance and Adventure" of our fantasy life in the

Photo © Pat Clyne

tropics suddenly slammed head-on with an in-your-face, hard look at our own mortality. "Was it really worth it?" seemed to be the unrelenting and distressing question that persistently plagued everyone. "No, of course not!" we thought, "Nothing's worth that! But it happened, and now we have to live with it." When reporters hounded Mel for a comment, all he would graciously say was, "It's a big ocean. It takes ships and people." But Mel was not about to let his oldest son's dream die with him.

Dirk had always said, "If we ever find a bronze cannon, it would show us the way to the rest of the *Atocha*." Dirk had just led his crew to nine of them. The search would go on! So, with newfound determination, borne from this tragic personal

> "It's a big ocean. It takes ships and people."
>
> — MEL FISHER

Mel Fisher oversees dredging work on the *Arbutus*. **(above)**

Kim Fisher, wife Jo-Arden and two of their three sons (Sean, now company VP, is on his mom's shoulders). **(above)**

Hugh Spinney on *Arbutus* **(above top)**

loss, the Fisher family along with the rest of us would find the *Atocha*, and we would do it in Dirk's name.

A NEW BEGINNING

Mel knew that even he was powerless over the forces of Mother Nature. But he could control the ways in which he could better protect his crew against those forces. Mel sold the company's remaining tugboat, *Southwind*, and he and then-vice president Bob Moran went to Miami and purchased a steel hull 179-foot former Coast Guard buoy tender, the *Arbutus,* which was to permanently stand guard over the wreck site. He converted one of the staterooms into a fully equipped first aid and medic station. He encouraged and even paid for crew members to take courses at the local college to learn the latest in first aid techniques should an emergency ever warrant it. He also hired a live-aboard licensed paramedic to accompany us on all our expeditions.

To this day, only speculation to the cause of the *Northwind's* sinking exists. No one really knows why it suddenly took on water that night and capsized so quickly. It's because of this inexplicable mystery that safeguards to prevent it from ever happening again seemed inadequate. Mel, nevertheless, was keenly aware of the unknown hazards on the sea and was determined to stave off any more fatalities on the site.

Hugh Spinney, a Bostonian with bravado, was in charge of getting the *Arbutus* seaworthy for a crew of at least a dozen divers. Hugh also captained the *Northwind* when Dirk was away at the Divers Training Academy and the *Southwind* when Kim moved to Michigan with his new wife, Jo-Arden, to study law. As an experienced diver, Hugh was eminently qualified for the task. After five months of retrofitting it for salvage work, the *Arbutus* was towed from Key West and anchored over the *Atocha* bronze cannons where it would remain a permanent on-site dive platform and crew's quarters. Tom Ford and I were chosen as captains for tours which lasted up to two weeks at a time on the wreck site.

The *Arbutus* was rigged with a large air compressor which powered several 20-foot-long, 10-inch diameter aluminum air-lifts that worked like underwater vacuum cleaners to clear away sand. Mel also had it equipped with a device called a Hydro-Flo that was actually a very large sump pump that was hydraulically raised and lowered into the water. This was an ingenious idea that basically brought Mel's mailbox technology down to the seabed to produce a powerful thrust of seawater directly onto the sandy overburden that needed to be removed.

This new calculated game plan not only created a large stable work platform for year-round diving activities but also fashioned around-the-clock vigilance over what was believed to be, at that time, Mel's "Big Pile." It was the fall of 1975 and the trail to the *Atocha* Motherlode from Dirk's recently discovered cannons was now underway.

NEW ADVERSARIES

Mel was very aware of how easily people could lose their rights when a few misguided government bureaucrats, driven by power and ambition, try to usurp those rights through unethical legislation. When the State of Florida became convinced that he was getting too close to finding all those riches, they decided that the *Atocha* really belonged to them. They now turned up the heat and began legal proceedings to take it away. Mel might have

Photo © Pat Clyne

Photo © Pat Clyne

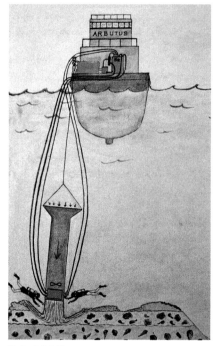

Photo © Pat Clyne

Sketch of how Hydra-Flo works **(above)**

Underwater shot of diver working the Hydra-Flo **(above left)**

Hydra-Flo being installed on the *Arbutus* **(left)**

Diver Tim March gets blown out over the water while trying to secure the boom. **(above)**

Diver Charlie Clyne drives whaler damaged during a storm. **(above top)**

Diver Steve Wickens rigs a pulley system for retrieving whaler. **(right)**

been "The World's Greatest Treasure Hunter" by profession, but he was also a student of the Constitution and he knew his rights. The former chicken farmer-turned-treasure hunter would fight for those rights with the same focused determination that he applied to his search for the *Atocha*.

The legal battles that ensued were expensive and took most of Mel's financial resources. Many times there wasn't enough money for food or fuel for the boats or paychecks for the divers and the office staff. But Mel's crew stayed on in spite of this. We had bought into Mel's dream years before, and we knew he was right; besides, we were still young, idealistic and lived for the adventure. Most of us already knew we were in it for the long haul. Since none of us could afford rent in downtown Key West, the salvage boats became our apartments and spearfishing replaced grocery shopping. Shared hard-times parties soon became more prevalent than the ribald Duval Street bar hopping scene. The adversity had drawn us closer and made us even more determined to help find Mel Fisher's "Big Pile."

Winter seasons were especially hard for us on the *Arbutus*. Heavy seas prevented supply boats from getting to the site to replenish dwindling provisions. Sometimes Mel didn't even have enough money to get the supply boat out of the harbor. But food wasn't the biggest issue for us. Out of pure necessity we all became spearfishing experts and gourmet cooks. If you were a seafood lover, you would have eaten better than you would have at most Key West restaurants. Of course you had to get used to lobster omelets for breakfast, grouper filets for lunch and a pot-ful of seafood jambalaya for dinner—not too shabby a cuisine for people who didn't own a dime.

The winter months also brought unusually heavy seas that would frequently crash over the bow and through the gunnels. Many times the *Arbutus* dive ladder was rendered useless and dangerous for any divers getting in or out of the water, but this was remedied by winching our port side into the oncoming sea, allowing a lee on the dive ladder's starboard side. The biggest problem for us was running out of fuel for the compressors and generators. They kept our scuba tanks filled and supplied air to our airlifts for digging, as well as our electrical equipment which charged our batteries, kept our refrigerator working and operated our radios which were our only link to Key West and the "real world."

Photo © Pat Clyne

Many times we faced a total blackout on the *Arbutus*. We cooked fish on the deck instead of the stove; we drank only the water that we had left, sometimes from melted ice in our coolers; we saved what fuel we could for our air tanks just to keep searching. To say that our crew had to become resourceful is a great understatement. We scavenged and cleaned rusted parts from old machinery found in the bowels of the ship just to keep other (just as old), machinery working. We built just about everything we needed from scratch, and because of the ship's constant need for repair, everyone learned to weld and cut steel as well as take apart and rebuild other outdated equipment. I guess it might be said (and it has), that our ship was a floating junkyard with a crew of rather eclectic divers who were trying

Photo © Pat Clyne

Arbutus winter dive apparel (Diver "Bouncy" John Lewis) **(above)**

Arbutus crew pose for "family" picture. Left to right: Tim March; Tommy Thomson; Dave Palmidor; Charlie Clyne; Don Jonas; Joe Spangler; Tom Ford. **(above left)**

Photo courtesy Fisher Family Collection

Mel Fisher's office was in a
replica Spanish galleon called the
Golden Doubloon. **(above)**

to turn rust into gold. But like I said earlier, the impossible would take us a little longer.

As always, Mel's family was a source of great inspiration for him. They all pooled their resources and did whatever needed to be done. Mel's daughter Taffi, now fourteen, and already a stunning beauty with the obvious good looks of her mom, would round up her high school girlfriends and man the company gift shop aboard Mel's replica Spanish galleon docked in Key West Harbor. They would sell tickets, give tours and try to interest tourists into buying coins from the 1715 fleet. The money raised would go for supplies and fuel to send the boats back out to the site.

Mel also hired some very attractive young women who dressed in short pirate outfits to lead tourists through our Spanish galleon museum. One in particular was a tall, stunning platinum blond with perfectly straight hair cascading down and around her shoulders. Sherry Vargas (now Sherry Culpepper), could have been a runway supermodel had Mel not convinced her that treasure hunting was much more rewarding with less chance of breaking one's heel on a catwalk. Sherry's big smile and gracious attitude had more than one customer—men and women, come back to our galleon gift shop to buy another coin or piece of jewelry. Sherry also helped fuel a lot of boats back out to that wreck site.

The company accountant, whose almost-impossible job it was to keep track of all the bills, IOUs and the occasional paycheck, was Marjory Hargreaves, or "TT" as everyone called her. The only thing harder than TT's job was cleaning the bilges and most of us would rather do that than answer angry calls from creditors. In spite of that, TT's daughter, Karen came to work for us helping her mom navigate in the sea of red ink in which we always seemed to find ourselves. David Hargreaves, Karen's brother, also crewed with us on many trips to make it a complete family affair.

Of course, throughout all of this, Mel's closest ally and confidante was Deo. Not only was she always by his side with words of support and encouragement, she also shared her caring insight with all the crew. Often she would pen personal notes thanking us for the work we were doing or complementing us on the work we had done. These personal little hand-written sentiments truly kept many of us going through these hard times.

For the following four years, the *Arbutus* crews continued to search for a new trail that would lead us from the cannons to the *Atocha* Motherlode, but all leads seemed to take us to a dead end. Even when two lone silver bars were recovered in 1978 on a "coral plateau," the trail eventually dwindled away, dashing our hopes again for that year. The State of Florida was still dragging Mel through the courts for the rights to the *Atocha*, trying to corrode his resolve along with his finances. Although they seemed to be succeeding in the latter, Mel's resolve was as strong as ever. They would take Mel to court over 100 times and over 100 times he would beat them, but by 1980 his finances had reached a new low. Even his persistent optimism couldn't ward off the expanding list of creditors.

Four years after the *Arbutus* arrived on site, many of their crew found that time wasn't any longer on their side. Most were now in their thirties, and with idealism turning into hard reality, the search for Mel's elusive dream became even more evasive. Those that had families were the first to look for paying jobs. Some just overcame their wanderlust for adventure or had acquired enough tales for years of story telling. After all, bragging rights for real treasure hunters comes with a price, and these guys and gals had paid dearly.

In 1979, less than a handful were left out of dozens of divers. By this time my co-captain, Tom Ford and I saw our crews dwindle down to only two or three crewmembers per tour. My younger brother Charlie joined the search in 1974 right out of high school. He was initiated as a "fryboy," crewed the yellow tugboats and endured several years on the *Arbutus*. He now became, on many occasions, my only companion aboard ship. With bad winter storms, little supplies and no foreseeable end to our legal problems, our times at sea were becoming more and more intolerable. However, in retrospect, and on a more personal note, I've learned more about him during those hard

Photo © Pat Clyne

Crewmember constructs scaffolding on *Arbutus* crane. **(above)**

Photo © Pat Clyne

Taffi Fisher displays gold chains in pool with nephews (Kim's sons) Jeremy and Sean. **(above)**

times than I ever would have known otherwise; the courage that he had shown during those years, would in the years to come, test his fortitude in the most challenging way possible, and again his courage would prevail.

ATOCHA'S SISTER SHIP—1980

As dawn broke over the Marquesas Islands, a *Virgalona* diver, shaking off sleep's foggy grip, staggered to the stern of the boat to relieve himself. As he looked down into the calm still water just before a cascade of ripples broke his mirror reflection, he noticed how clearly he could see every contour and blade of grass on the bottom. It was not unusual for the water visibility to be clear in the Florida Keys, but some days in the summer, it was truly spectacular.

After a quick breakfast of coffee, eggs and sausage, the anchor was pulled, and the crew of the *Virgalona* was under way for another day on the *Atocha* trail. As their streamlined bow cut through the glassy surface of the water, the shadow of their boat could be seen slithering across the seabed 30 feet below. One of the divers sitting on the stern couldn't take his eyes off of the frequently changing bottom features. And it turned out to be a good thing someone was watching. A half-hour into their voyage, he spotted something that triggered a scream to the captain, "Hey Mo, turn this boat around—*quick!*"

While Mo was swinging the huge wooden wheel hard to the right, the diver was already gearing up. Before the *Virgalona* could even come to a complete stop, he was in the water racing toward the sandy bottom. All eyes followed the silver stream of bubbles to the bottom where they could make out his silhouette gliding across what appeared to be railroad ties. After a few more minutes, he was breaking the water shouting, "Timbers, there's ship timbers down there!" Although it is a well-known fact that most submerged wood in the tropics disappears after a few decades, sometimes it can be preserved if it is buried deep enough in the sand. The area the divers were in was known as the Quicksands because of its constantly changing bottom features. The *Virgalona* just "happened" to pass right over these

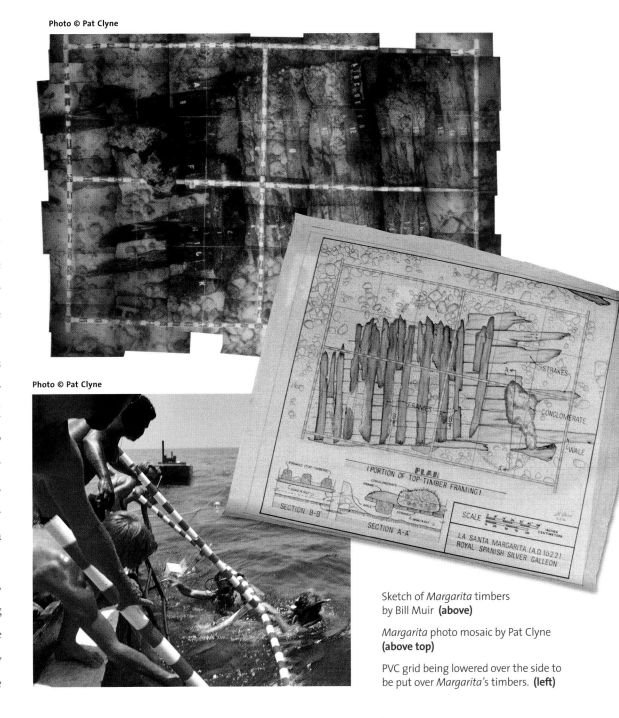

timbers at the time they just "happened" to be exposed and on a day the visibility just "happened" to be at its best while someone just "happened" to be looking over the side. Just what are the odds that could have "happened?" Actually, no one really cared. It looked like Mel's divers had just found themselves the remains of a Spanish galleon. But was it part of the *Atocha*?

Word was sent back to Key West and a full expedition was mounted. Since the *Arbutus* had been decomissioned just a few months before, the company had only the *Virgalona* left. Mel subcontracted other salvage boats with mailbox "technology" to work the new site. Shortly after a light dusting with the mailboxes, silver coins began appearing throughout the site. Soon, 80-pound silver bars were being located, then gold bars followed with gold chains by the handful. This was absolutely a high-ranking shipwreck laden with precious cargo.

A PVC underwater grid was made to fit over the timbers, and I constructed a portable photo-trac to create overlapping photographs to form a continuous photo mosaic of the entire structure. A full underwater archaeological project was now underway. There was no doubt that it was a ship in the *Atocha*

Sketch of *Margarita* timbers by Bill Muir **(above)**

Margarita photo mosaic by Pat Clyne **(above top)**

PVC grid being lowered over the side to be put over *Margarita*'s timbers. **(left)**

Curator Leah Miguel studies gold links as artist Larissa Dillon sketches artifacts. **(above)**

Mel Fisher and archaeologist Jim Sinclair view set of silver nested cups. **(above right)**

fleet, but its distance from the known-*Atocha* trail varied greatly. Mel, who had always relied heavily on Gene Lyon's research, consulted the scholar once more to find the answer. According to archival documents of the Spanish survivors, the *Santa Margarita* sailors told a tale of having watched from the decks of their own doomed vessel as the once-majestic *Atocha*, fatally damaged, rose for the last time on a mighty wave only to slide down the other side into the raging sea. Shortly after, the *Margarita* was to meet the same fate. The documents that Dr. Lyon found, came to be an uncanny accurate measurement of the *Santa Margarita*'s distance from the *Atocha*'s actual resting place. The distance translated into approximately three nautical miles. The indication, it seemed, was that Mel's team had just located the second largest treasure-laden galleon in the 1622 fleet, the *Atocha*'s sister ship—*Santa Margarita*. And if Gene Lyon's research was correct, the *Atocha* might just be only three miles away.

The new decade of the '80s was indeed starting out well. The news media was all over Mel and the world was beginning to see some beautiful things being recovered from this historic ship. Mel's status as "The World's Greatest Hunter" grew by leaps and bounds.

The *Santa Margarita* expedition continued in earnest for two more years. Duncan Mathewson brought in a new, young bright archaeologist by the name of Jim Sinclair whose conservation work helped Mel's company usher in a whole new awareness of the explorers of our continent centuries ago. Mel knew that there was more work to do on the *Margarita*, but for him, it was imperative to tie the whole story of the lost 1622 fleets together and he wasn't able to do that without the *Atocha*.

Of course the only obstacle left right now that would prevent Mel from accomplishing any of this was that small matter of the State of Florida still wanting to take it all away. Mel had now been in and out of the federal courts for over seven years battling for his right of ownership of these shipwrecks, and it now finally came down to only one court left that would hear and ultimately decide the fate of these ships.

Mel had put together an excellent legal defense team. Bleth McHaley, a brilliant public relations director from California, had become his vice president and paralegal liaison in matters concerning law. David Paul Horan, a Key West attorney and diver, became so absorbed in Mel's legal battle, that when he eventually realized he was on the same pay scale as the rest of us (which pretty much meant pro bono), he still continued the fight. But David Paul was about to take a journey into the world of jurisprudence that would slingshot him into the hallowed halls of the Supreme Court of the United States. Law Professor

William Vandercreek was about to witness Horan, his student and protégée, argue Mel's case before those nine justices and succeed in setting a precedent in U.S. law that would protect individuals from intrusive government meddling in their livelihood. The search for the famed ship, *Atocha* that began 11 years earlier was about to take on, once again, a whole new legal perspective with Mel's stunning victory in the Supreme Court.

THE NEW SEARCH

By 1982, Mel had four new salvage vessels: a large steel hull ship called *J.B. Magruder* captained by Donny Jonas, a former Navy crew boat called *Swordfish*, captained by Tom Ford, a reliable ocean-going tugboat named *Dauntless*, a fiberglass cabin cruiser named the *Bookmaker* and of course the *Virgalona*, which remained one of the company's most reliable workhorses.

Mel and Deo's son, Kim, former captain of the old yellow tug *Southwind*, had just returned from Michigan where he spent a few years studying law. But the family business was always first and foremost on his mind. Kim was now at the helm of the *Bookmaker*. The former luxurious cabin cruiser was gutted of its

Kim Fisher's search vessel, the *Bookmaker* (above)

Former VP Bleth McHaley working with attorney David Paul Horan on legal documents for our Supreme Court hearing (above top)

Salvage boats anchored over *Atocha*'s main pile (*Virgalona*, *Swordfish* and *Dauntless*) (left)

Kane Fisher uses winch to set stern anchors. **(above)**

Diver surfaces through a bed of Sargassa weed (sea grass). **(opposite page; top left)**

Surface view of airlift operations on *Atocha* site **(opposite page; top right)**

Kane Fisher on the trail **(opposite page; bottom right)**

amenities and was outfitted with the latest marine search detection equipment. Kim would take the *Bookmaker* back to the *Atocha* trail and begin again to pursue its elusive scatter pattern.

Kane Fisher was now in his early twenties and had already proven his proficiency as a salvage master by his work on the *Margarita*. Mel made him captain of the powerful tugboat *Dauntless* and also assigned him to the *Atocha* site. However, this didn't take much coaxing as Kane's whole psyche was already fixated on what needed to be done. As Kim and his *Bookmaker* crew detected potential targets on the sea floor, Kane would anchor the *Dauntless* over the hit and dig through centuries of sand to identify it. Occasionally he would find something that would indicate they were on the right trail, but 99 percent of the hits were modern trash. The area that the *Atocha* trail was in was also a Navy target range so invariably most of the metal targets were exploded bombs, and yes, even some unexploded ones, which predictably brought back the crew's slogan of "cheatin' death" again.

The long, hot, scorching days on the trail turned into months, then years. By 1985, it would seem that Mel was no closer to finding the rest of the *Atocha* than he was since the last silver bar recoveries on the *Arbutus* in 1977. It was now almost three years since we had seen any significant treasure surface from the *Margarita*. Many of us would end up going back to the "Bank of Spain" before returning to port. One could always find a few more coins scattered in the sand and none of us wanted to come back "skunked" after a ten-day trip at sea.

Most everyone by this time was beginning to grow a little weary, again. It was now over sixteen years since Mel started his search. Many of the newer divers and crew hired after the *Arbutus* found themselves leaving and going back to the "real world." Just a few of the original crew from the early '70s were still on board. But anyone passing Mel's office would never think there were any setbacks. One could hear Mel on the phone telling people why he was sure that "Today was the Day!" This phrase he used daily with his crew and investors. It was an intense prophetical belief that if he could dream it, he could do it. That part was never questioned by anyone who knew him.

Kane Fisher not only shared his father's dream, as did all of the family, but he seemed mesmerized with a very private incentive to carry on the *Atocha* expedition. Kane was on the boat when his brother Dirk had lost his life to the quest, and he felt it was up to him personally to make sure it wasn't in vain. While many of the other salvage boats were working farther north on the trail closer to where the cannons were found, Kane kept pushing further and further to the southeast. Month after month he would find some small clue and keep heading in that direction. By now it had become known as Kane's trail. By the spring of 1985, Kane was almost nine miles to the southeast of the cannon site—so far away that most outsiders, and even some insiders, thought he and his crew had baked in the sun far too long and it had affected their thinking. But he couldn't care less what other people thought. He had his father's resolve and his brother's doggedness, and as far as he was concerned, that's all that was needed.

On July 19th, 1985, Kane's trail extended almost ten miles away from where the search began. But unlike hundreds of other days on the trail, that day would be different. That day they would find ballast stones, barrel hoops and various other encrusted objects, which were more shipwreck artifacts than had been found in years. The further down the trail they went, the more

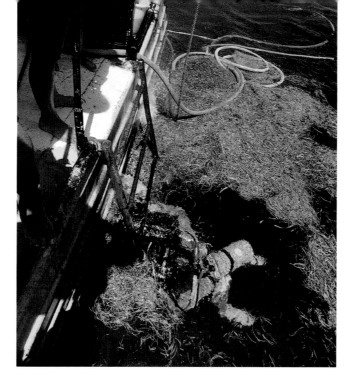

Photo © Pat Clyne

Photo © Pat Clyne

Photo © Pat Clyne

The tourists who gather to participate are told fables by the local native high priests, or panhandlers, again depending on how much you're willing to believe, of ye ol' pirate lore of what happens when you spot the green flash. It is said that upon the witness of the flash, "souls of the dead will return to the world of the living." And it must be true; Captain Jack Sparrow believed it, didn't he?

wreckage they found. They were coming into something significant, and they could all sense it, but none more than Kane. It seemed as though he was now being guided by pure instinct, or was it something even more intuitive?

As the bright orange ball of sun dipped into the ocean just the other side of the horizon, all eyes were fixated on one tiny spot on top of that bright sphere. Would they catch the green flash in that wisp of a second, which is just enough time to see it, or think they saw it? This phenomenon, or folklore, depending on how much you're willing to believe, is practiced in a nightly ritual at Key West's Mallory Square at every sunset.

That same night during that same sunset 30 miles away, the crew of the *Dauntless* watched too, as the sun slowly dissolved into the sea around them. They anchored over the site that night … if, in fact, it was the *Atocha's* final resting place. How many of them would doze off to sleep under the stars thinking of those 260 souls who lost their lives on this Spanish galleon? How many would contemplate their last agonizing moments as the ferocious waves dragged them to their watery graves? Who among them would admit to seeing the green flash that night?

The next morning, July 20th, 1985, Kane got the crew up early for breakfast. He seemed even more methodical than usual. Like an actor who had diligently rehearsed hitting his mark over and over, he went through his routine shouting commands to his men in the Boston whaler as they set the ship's large stern anchors, calling out position as they winched in the heavy wet anchor line, ordering certain divers to gear up. Kane seemed to have suddenly found a direct focus; it was like something was propelling him from within as he orchestrated every movement of his men and ship.

After the boat was positioned precisely where Kane's latest instincts determined, he sent two of his divers, Andy Matroci and Greg Wareham, over the side. Each carried metal detec-

tors which they switched on immediately after settling on the bottom 55 feet below their ship. Greg signaled that he was going to search to the north. Andy would go west. It wasn't long before Greg's metal detector began clicking. In a sweeping motion, Greg started to follow the signal as it became stronger. The clicking became more rapid as he kicked his fins harder toward the increasing pulse. Greg took his eyes off the head of his detector to look up, but the visibility was cloudy and he couldn't see but a few feet in front of him. He kept kicking. By now, his detector was no longer giving off telltale clicks; it was shrieking a high-pitched scream. Looking up again, through the haze, he could make out a rise on the bottom, like a hump. He pointed his detector in that direction. Never had it yelled back at him so loudly.

Andy too, was beginning to get hits on his detector, only they were dying out the further west he went. So he traced it around to the north until the pulse began to pick up. Like Greg, his signals started going off the scale the closer he approached the same hump. Greg, getting closer, could now begin to see dark angular shapes forming from the dark mass in front of him; he

Andy Matroci and Greg Wareham show off an intact clump of over 2,000 "pieces of eight." **(above)**

Silver bars underwater on *Atocha* site **(left)**

Left to right: Don Jonas, Mel Fisher, Kane Fisher and R. D. LeClair show off some of the day's gold recovery. **(above)**

Divers holding silver bars, left to right: Spencer Wickens, Curtis White, "Big Rig" Chuck Sotzin, R. D. LeClair, Jerry Cash and "Cocktail" Bill Reighard **(above top)**

Mel Fisher holding peanut jar containing hundreds of emeralds while diver Ed Hinkle holds two gold discs with Dave Jonas in background **(right)**

kicked harder. His heart was pounding so loudly he thought it was his metal detector.

Andy was approaching the same shapes and was now able to see Greg in front and to the right of him. Greg glanced over and spotted Andy coming out of the haze. They both stopped and just stared at each other, both wondering if the other was thinking the same thing. Greg pointed, Andy nodded, and they both started kicking towards the rapidly forming shapes. Seconds later, both Andy and Greg swam into 17th-century Spain, frozen in time on the ocean bottom.

Darkened and encrusted, the divers immediately recognized the silver bars that were stacked like cordwood two and three feet high, just as they were stacked hundreds of years ago. According to the *Atocha*'s manifest, she was carrying over a thousand of these large bars, and the scene before their eyes, as far as they could see, seemed to verify that they were all still there. Andy couldn't keep this "secret" to himself any longer and shot to the surface to report to his captain. Kane was in the wheelhouse on the third deck when Andy broke the surface and started shouting that they had the "Big Pile" and that it was all laying right there.

With the noise of the engines running and the loud compressors pushing air into scuba tanks, Kane couldn't understand a word Andy was saying, but he didn't have to. It was written all over his face. With that cue, Kane jumped from the third deck to the second and then second to the first. He put on a mask and fins and grabbed a tank as he went over the side.

Kane kicked hard to reach the bottom and swam to the area where Andy had surfaced. The visibility was improving, and by the time Kane arrived, he could see the outlines of many stacks of silver bars. Rising up a few more feet from the bottom to get a better bird's-eye view of the area, Kane could now begin to see the immensity of the site. He began to kick softly, gliding across the visible remains of the hull of the ship that he had been looking for most of his life. As he slowly drifted across this magnificent scene, Kane was suddenly struck with two very powerful and intense emotions. One was the tremendous satisfaction of having been vindicated by extending the trail, as well as finding "The Motherlode of the *Atocha*," exactly what his dad had been so determined to discover. His other emotion was no less intense. The date also raced through his mind.

It was July 20th 1985, exactly ten years to the day that Kane had been abruptly awakened in the middle of the night and tossed into the sea with the remainder of the *Northwind* crew. It was ten years ago that his brother Dirk had drowned.

Kane swam to the surface, his mind churning with mixed emotions, but mostly with the satisfaction that he had succeeded in making his dad's dream come true. As he swam on the surface to the *Dauntless* dive ladder, he could vaguely hear his crew onboard cheering. But Kane was now totally absorbed in thought; he was suddenly experiencing a higher plane of consciousness and he knew right then that he was not alone. He was having an existential moment, one that not only sustained him for all those years but the same one which guided his hand in the search. Some would say it was just the intense exhilaration of the moment, but Kane, and a few others, knew better.

Kane scaled the dive ladder and with all his gear still on climbed to the third deck. Soaking wet, he reached into the wheelhouse, picked up the radio microphone and hailed his dad's office in Key West. "Put away the charts, Dad; we've got the Motherlode!" was all that needed to be said.

Mel's longtime personal secretary Judy Gracer on the left with accountant Sandy Dunn, pick out some of their personal favorite gold pieces. **(above)**

Diver/photographer Damien Lin holds a smattering of gold just recovered. **(above top)**

Photo © Pat Clyne

Photo © Pat Clyne

Mel Fisher holding gold ingots and an ornate serving plate from the *Atocha* **(above)**

Archaeologist Duncan Mathewson checks gold and silver bar numbers from copy of *Atocha*'s manifest. Diver Mike Mayer holds gold bars. **(above right)**

After centuries of abandonment on the ocean bottom, the remains of the *Atocha*'s lower hull section, which carried the bulk of the 47 tons of listed silver and gold, had finally been located. Over a thousand silver bars, weighing an average of 85 pounds each, were raised, along with hundreds of gold bars. Most were carrying their maker's mark, which, for historians and archaeologists, was the real treasure gleaned from this discovery. Experts in many other disciplines were also astonished at the incredible amount of significant information this ship was now generating.

Mel and archaeologist Duncan Mathewson could see the educational value in this great discovery. So word went out to academic institutions all over the world to join us in helping to study these wonderful pieces of history. Unfortunately, many in the archaeological community, fearing recrimination from their peers by giving Mel Fisher's work legitimacy, opted not to accept the invitation.

Those that knew Mel and his family knew they had always stressed the educational and preservation value of their finds. Even when Mel's most vocal critics would claim he was "destroying" history, the insiders knew the truth. If it hadn't been for Mel, this history would still be rotting under the sea. Mel was doing all along what many of his envious critics wished they could be doing, and by most accounts, doing it better.

Photo © Pat Clyne

Photo © Pat Clyne

Photo © Pat Clyne

Taffi Fisher holds out *Atocha* gold bars. **(above)**

Mel and Kane Fisher congratulate and toast the crew on *Atocha* site. **(above top)**

Memorial Day find—divers left to right: Andy Matroci, Sterling Rivers, Bill Barron, Susan Nelson, Fay Field, Mel Fisher and Jim Sinclair **(left)**

Dreamweaver Turns Folk Hero

Many of us were experiencing a bittersweet satisfaction. After all those years, we had become accustomed to and settled into searching for the *Atocha*. The daily routine of moving our ships a few more yards along the trail, turning on the mailboxes and diving into another empty hole now seemed to be a thing of the past. Overnight, our status went from "treasure hunters" to "treasure finders." Although we all believed that one day we would find it, still, not one person was actually prepared for that day to happen, not even Mel Fisher.

"*N*ow what do we do?" laughed Mel as he looked into my video camera lens. That became the question most asked among the crew and staff. Some even felt that maybe it meant their job was now over. However, an essential lesson in marketing, advertising and public relations was about to be learned by all. The *Atocha* and the Mel Fisher story would take on a whole new persona in the eyes of the world, not only in the media, but also on the political scene. Whole new generations of people were learning of Mel's exploits and his indomitable spirit, optimism and patriotism in the face of some incredible odds. What started out as one man's search for treasure was now being written about in history books and added to academic curriculums. It soon became apparent that not only were Mel's people not going to lose their jobs but that the staff needed to be increased just to facilitate the ever-increasing legend behind the man— Mel Fisher.

Almost six months after the Motherlode was discovered, wonderful things were still being found. Divers working the airlifts in the sand on the outer perimeter of the *Atocha*'s timbers suddenly hit a pocket of uncut emeralds which were immedi-

ately sucked up the lift and abruptly blown from the top of the 20-foot aluminum vacuum tube. Looking up, we could see a shower of little green crystal rocks falling down on us. Like kids catching fireflys at night, we stood upright on the bottom plucking emeralds from the water as quickly as they plummeted back down.

This was certainly a surprise to most of us who by now practically memorized the *Atocha*'s manifest and knew nothing like this was ever mentioned. It had to be contraband! We all guessed the emeralds that were now being found by the hundreds had to have been smuggled aboard the Spanish galleon. But it was no surprise to Mel who now had us cap off the top of the airlifts with long extension tubes leading back up to the deck of the salvage

Photo © Pat Clyne

Media frenzy over Mel Fisher's
Atocha discovery **(right)**

Divers pulling up cart from left
to right: "Shaky" Jake Viscum,
Steve Swindell and Greg Wareham.
(opposite page; right)

The sudden shock of finding the *Atocha*'s Motherlode after all these years caught everyone unprepared. For the divers, this sudden and massive adrenaline rush meant that somehow they could swim theses 85-pound silver bars to the surface. Like the bumblebee who is unaware that he's aerodynamically unfit to fly, they did what gravity shouldn't have allowed them to do. Before the end of the day, they radioed in their predicament. The crewmembers who were still in port, biting at the bit to get out there, solved the problem. That night they went over to the local supermarket parking lot and "borrowed" a few shopping carts to bring out the next day. They worked brilliantly!

Point of interest to shoppers: These carts can only hold four silver bars at a time.

Panning for emeralds **(above)**

Rare Colombian emeralds in a bed of
Atocha gold chain **(above right)**

boats. With the ocean's bottom now being spewed out on the deck, we could search through the sand for these emeralds with food strainers and dust pans swiped from the galley.

Mel, with his experience in panning for gold, soon developed a device similar to the shaker tables used in the Klondike. All of us went to work building tables, not to find gold, but to locate smuggled green gems. Working with Mel for so long, we were not strangers to his ingenuity and innovation. So his invention, with a little tweaking, worked just fine. The extension tube from the airlift was connected to a large box sitting on a makeshift table on the ship's deck. When the airlift was working, water and sand was pumped up through the box which separated the big shells and allowed the sand and water to flow down to a long table covered with a screen mesh. We would line up on both sides and sift the sand with plastic dustpans by pushing the examined overburden down the table and back into the ocean. At any given moment you might hear someone yell, "I got another one!" This would continue all day as we eventually recovered some of the world's most beautiful uncut Colombian emeralds ever seen.

Mel would use this emerald recovery technique to encourage those investors who didn't dive to go out to the site. More than anything else he wanted to share with them the actual experience of the "hunt." He had always let his dive-certified investors work alongside his men and would love to hear their stories when they got back to port. Now, he reasoned, everyone could experience the "Fun, Romance and Adventure" of the search and not even get wet. What could be better than former armchair adventurers getting out of those chairs and finding their own treasure? What stories they could bring home! The investors loved it, and they loved him for making it possible. Mel Fisher was becoming America's "Dreamweaver."

The *Atocha*'s lower hull section by this time had been almost completely documented. Grids and transect lines could be seen wherever you went on the site. Captain Syd Jones and his wife, K.T., spent countless hours meticulously sketching artifact location in relation to timber placement of the hull and produced the most comprehensive site drawing to date. K.T. also researched and wrote a booklet on the coins of the *Atocha*; a publication that is regarded, in some circles, as the definitive word on *Atocha* and *Margarita* coins.

FAME AND OTHER NECESSARY BAGGAGE

By 1986, Mel Fisher's celebrity had become a worldwide phenomenon of sorts. Producers of the late night TV talk shows sought him out. He was a favorite on *The Tonight Show Starring Johnny Carson* as he went one-on-one with the quick-witted comedian. When Johnny asked him how many hundreds of millions of dollars he thought was on the *Atocha*, Mel deadpanned, "I'm not quite sure of the total, but it might just cover your alimony payments." This caused the audience and the late night host to break up so badly, he was forced to cut to

commercial. When they returned it was obvious Mel was on a roll. Amidst all the gold bars, discs and chains he was showing Carson, a rather mundane object caught his host's eye. It was a long cylindrical bronze artifact that had been used by the ship's physician as a tool by which to administer enemas. Not knowing what to make of this strange non-glittering object, Johnny began to quiz the treasure hunter on what it was used for. Mel, who couldn't resist the straight line, replied, "Bend over and I'll show ya."

Before the show ended, the two had seemed to form a friendly bond. Johnny mentioned, on air, that he was a scuba diver and had a vacation coming up. Mel, not missing the hint, invited him to come on down and help him find some more treasure. A few weeks later, 30 miles west of Key West, a fast formula boat pulled up to the *J.B. Magruder* and *Dauntless*. A smiling Mel Fisher disembarked and began introducing his latest TV personality friend to the crew. Johnny and Mel soon geared up and took the plunge down to the *Atocha*'s remains as *National Geographic* and I filmed the entire dive. Johnny Carson presented the film clips on *The Tonight Show* to millions of viewers

Photo © Pat Clyne

Syd Jones sketches *Atocha*'s timbers in relation to artifacts found. **(above)**

showing him and "The World's Greatest Treasure Hunter" combing the famed Spanish galleon for yet more "pieces of history."

Not only was America enthralled with Mel Fisher's exploits, his fame seemed to extend far beyond its borders. Requests for personal appearances came in from around the world. One such request was from the national TV station in Rome. RAI Rome broadcasted a six-hour variety show and flew Mel, Deo and I first class from Key West. There were three days of rehearsals leading to a production no less amazing than a Hollywood extravaganza—Italian style.

After the very successful airing of the show, we were all given a tour of the Vatican and St. Peter's Basilica. Because of the TV special, Mel was now being recognized all over Rome, sometimes in the most unlikely places. While we walked together through one of the many arched marble alcoves, a statuesque Swiss Guard

Rome, Italy—Mel Fisher on the set of an Italian variety show **(above left)**

Johnny Carson and Mel Fisher on *Atocha* site **(above right)**

Mel Fisher, Deo Fisher, Pat Clyne and Taffi Fisher celebrate the *Atocha* at Caesars Palace, Las Vegas. **(right)**

standing sentry and perfectly still with lance firmly in hand, suddenly recognized Mel as he and Deo walked by. Ordinarily, these guards are trained never to flinch under any circumstances, but it appeared as though this one might have missed Swiss Guard school that day. His following eyes finally gave way to a sudden eager outburst of, "Feesher? Mr. Feesher?" Mel and Deo stopped, surprised by the unexpected recognition by such an unlikely fan. They smiled, and at the guard's request, gave him an autograph. If Mel Fisher had any semblance of anonymity before, it seemed as though those days were now over.

As expected, Hollywood came knocking. There were a number of production companies vying for the rights to "The Mel Fisher Story," some offering significant sums for those rights. Mel turned them all down. Early on in his career, Mel became aware of the significance of maintaining the "rights" to his life and the stories surrounding it. Although he would encourage and even promote the availability of his life to filmmakers, it would always be on a nonexclusive basis. Nobody was going to "own" Mel Fisher. To him, it was a slippery slope towards relinquishing control of what he did, and Mel did whatever Mel wanted to do,

whenever he wanted to do it. Even when the Disney Corporation wanted in, Mel said *no* to the world's most influential rodent.

So, when a film production company came to him with the idea of a two-hour docudrama for CBS where he would be paid a flat fee and keep the rights to his story, Mel agreed. Filming of *Dreams of Gold, The Mel Fisher Story* began in 1986 in the Virgin Islands of St. Croix. For five weeks, the Fisher family divided their time between the Caribbean and Key West getting to know their alter-ego characters and volunteering as story consultants. CBS hired academy award-winning actor, Cliff Robertson to play Mel Fisher and Loretta Swit ("Hotlips" from the TV show, *Mash*) to play Deo Fisher. The Fisher children were played by a notable ensemble of movie and TV personalities.

Of course, Hollywood being known more for its glitzy presentations than portraying the facts, produced an action-packed, fast-paced account of Mel and his family's exploits that at least maintained the theme and gist of Mel's expeditions, if not the accurate details.

Like some tabloid journalists who maintain the adage of not letting the facts get in the way of a good story, *Dreams of Gold*

Photo © Pat Clyne

Photo © Pat Clyne

Loretta Swit and Deo Fisher on set of *Dreams of Gold* in St. Croix **(above)**

Mel Fisher and Cliff Robertson on set of *Dreams of Gold* in St. Croix **(above top)**

For the filming of *Dreams of Gold* in St. Croix, are two replicas of *Northwind*—one overturned in foreground to duplicate the sinking scene and one working model in background. **(above left)**

Loretta Swit poses with Hollywood's version of the *Atocha* treasure. **(above right)**

Cinematographer Nick Calyonis films segment for CBS's docudrama, *Dreams of Gold* **(right)**

was filmed in the fashion that the producers felt would live up to the Hollywood image. An example would be their portrayal of what the *Atocha*'s Motherlode looked like. After viewing hours of the underwater footage that I filmed on the actual site, they felt it didn't look shiny enough. So their prop department proceeded to cut up hundreds of wooden two-by-four planks in two-foot segments, sprayed them gold and sprinkled glitter on them as an added touch before they nailed them all together. These were supposed to represent stacks of gold bars that Mel's crew had found and were to be placed on the underwater movie set for the big "Motherlode" finale scene. However, no one seemed to recall at the time that wood actually floats when immersed in water. So instead of stacks of gold bars on the ocean bottom, they had several very impressive bright twinkling wooden rafts—not exactly what the directors had in mind.

The quick-thinking prop staff immediately came up with the solution and headed to the nearest hardware store to purchase several yards of cyclone fencing. This was attached to the glittering wooden rafts successfully weighing them to the bottom

where they rested in the sand looking exactly like a stack of gold painted two-by-fours. Nevertheless, this seemed to please the director who also placed large iron treasure chests overflowing with plastic gold chains held down with gold painted rocks and an assortment of other imitation glitzy jewels. In spite of the many liberties taken with the story, the Fishers thoroughly enjoyed the experience of working on the set and sharing their exploits with all the actors and film crew.

In 1987 Mel and his family were the guests of honor at the premiere of *Dreams of Gold* at the Kennedy Fine Arts Center in Washington D.C. Mel was to speak to the large audience and accept an award by Willard Scott, whom he adorned with gold chain and proceeded to infect with "gold fever." A large black tie reception followed and Mel and Deo, once again, became the main attraction at an affair that raised tens of thousands of dollars for charity, something they did regularly.

BACK TO THE SEA

As always, Mel's interest returned to the sea and the secrets it held. Even though his divers were still recovering artifacts from

the *Atocha*, Mel began to look for other lost shipwrecks. For the next decade he would form a number of expeditions in this country as well as in the Caribbean and South America. Although many believed that there would never again be another "*Atocha*," Mel's perpetual optimism continued to astound people and his typical charismatic personality would induce many into accompanying him on his numerous adventures.

People would join him, not to get rich, but to be a part of the spirit that drives legendary figures to greatness. The search, many learned, was really the treasure after all. In searching, they would ultimately find themselves. The material wealth became secondary; the accomplishments, the camaraderie, the close relationships formed, all led to a much greater treasure hunt, and I think Mel knew that. Behind that smile and the ever-present twinkle in his eye, he knew that the treasure was a fleeting thing and just the means to an end—but friendship was forever.

Mel Fisher died on December 9th, 1998 and his ashes were returned back to the sea; the place where he knew most of the answers could be found and where many others would continue to explore and seek out their dreams, whatever they may be.

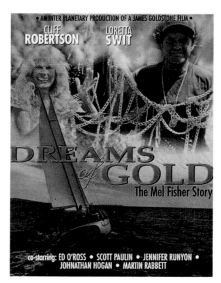

Poster and DVD cover of the CBS docudrama *Dreams of Gold* (above)

Mel Fisher adjusts *Dreams of Gold* cap on Willard Scott's head. (above top)

TODAY'S EXPLORERS

The Fisher family of treasure hunters continues to carry on their father's legacy to this day with Mel's children having leadership roles in all facets of their father's business. Mel's wife and lifetime partner, Dolores passed away in December of 2009. Deo, the matriarch of this treasure-hunting dynasty, continued to play a major role in the activities of the company that she and her husband began on their honeymoon many years ago when Mel promised her "Fun, Romance and Adventure"—a promise that did not go unfulfilled. It is, in large part, due to her tireless efforts and sincere concern for her family and employees that the company has succeeded in its quest for so many decades.

Kane moved back up to the Treasure Coast, the area on the east coast of Florida which inherited its namesake from his father's success on the shipwrecks of the 1715 fleet in the 1960s. There he continues to be involved in the shipwrecks that his dad's treasure-hunting career began with so many years before.

Mel's son by a former marriage, Terry, and his wife Carla, who had detected significant targets on both the *Atocha* and the *Margarita* trails, had moved to Arizona. Although they had always preferred a low-key approach to their occupation, they were nonetheless important contributors in the overall success of their family's quest. Terry has since relocated to Hawaii, to another tropical island that he had always loved.

Taffi Fisher, now Taffi Fisher-Abt, lives in Sebastian, Florida on a ranch with her husband Michael and their youngest son Melvin. Their ranch is appropriately named the M.T. Pockets Ranch. Although they will tell you that M and T stand for their initials, there's no doubt in the irony of the name and its possible origin.

Taffi is president of the Mel Fisher Center in Sebastian. A converted firehouse is now home to a breathtaking museum of fabulous treasures from the Spanish Fleet of 1715 as well as some of the *Atocha* and *Margarita* treasures. Taffi employs a modest museum staff as well as overseeing the conservation lab.

Taffi is also the director of the East Coast Shipwreck Project, an enormous responsibility that includes administrating as many as 50 subcontractors while dealing with state-sanctioned permits within a 35-mile stretch of Florida's coastline. This would be a daunting challenge for any one person to manage—but, of

course this isn't just any one person. Taffi is the product of her parents, two extraordinary adventurers gifted with an exceptional ability to believe in themselves and others. Taffi has also been an inspiration with her encouragement, advise and support to many "would-be treasure hunters" just starting out in the business. And like her mom, she's always able to make room in her heart for just one more person; a rare quality that is never lost on those fortunate enough to know her.

Taffi, and longtime associates Bill Moore and John Brandon, created extensive computer records by which all the locations and provenance of the 1715 fleet recoveries are compiled and documented; a monumental task taking almost a decade to construct. This impressed the State of Florida officials who have been trying to develop a similar database of their collection for many years and who now consult with the Fishers on their research.

Through Taffi's efforts and those of the Key West office, a ground-breaking achievement in research of historic shipwreck recoveries can now be shared with all people throughout the world. This database along with the one created for the *Atocha* artifacts were the world's first comprehensive online public shipwreck databases. This has been applauded in both the public and private sectors as a ground-breaking new research tool for the academic community, students or just plain admirers of maritime history. Now, scholars and pupils alike seeking research on the latest recoveries of Spanish antiquities can, for the first time, access it directly online from their computers.

Kim Fisher, no less talented a sibling, now directs the operations from his fourth floor office in the large brick building in Key West, which also houses the Mel Fisher Maritime Museum. Kim, who has since remarried, lives in Key West with his wife, Lee, and their two boys, Scott and Ricky. Kim's experience developed under his father's guidance made him the ideal choice as leader of the company's continued expeditions. After

Sebastian Museum **(above)**

Photo © Pat Clyne

his father's death, Kim assumed full-time responsibility of the company and continues to expand upon his father's exploits through the use of high-tech marine-search techniques. Kim has put together a team of experts whose combined efforts have made his crew today's leading underwater professionals in locating historical shipwrecks.

After graduating with a degree in marketing, Sean Fisher, one of Kim's three sons from his previous marriage to Jo-Arden, moved to Key West in 2005 with his wife Star. Sean, a father himself of two young future divers, Jack and Max, became the company's marketing director and media consultant. He immediately got to work promoting the Mel Fisher line of products as well as working with TV and movie producers for upcoming

media specials. Sean, like his relatives before him, was a professional diver, but he also carried a certification in mixed-gas diving for accessing those deeper wrecks that had, until now, been just out of reach for the family to safely consider. He has since become the company vice president and has already taken on a large part of the responsibilities. He will inevitably continue with his grandfather's legacy.

To complete the Fisher Dynasty, two of Taffi's four children, Joshua and Nichole, are also very much a part of the Fisher's home-grown business. Nichole, who has inherited both her grandmother and mother's beauty, now manages The Mel Fisher Museum in Sebastian. Nichole's older brother Joshua, moved

Photo © Pat Clyne

Kim, his wife Lee and their two boys,
Scott and Ricky, in the wheelhouse
(above)

Kim and son Sean on *Atocha* site **(right)**